when you can travel
within your own interior
there's definitely
no place like home

Homes for Nomads

Jan Verlinde &
Thijs Demeulemeester

interiors of the
well-travelled

Lannoo

'I'd rather have a passport full of stamps than a house full of stuff', you'll sometimes hear people with wanderlust say. Nice slogan for a coffee mug. But why not have your cake and eat it too? An interior can just as easily be an exciting travel story, can't it?

nl

'I'd rather have a passport full of stamps than a house full of stuff', hoor je mensen met reislust wel zeggen. Een mooie spreuk voor op een koffiemok, dat wel. Maar waarom zou het een het ander moeten uitsluiten? Een interieur kan toch evengoed een spannend reisverhaal zijn?

Kijk maar naar de 19 globetrotters die fotograaf Jan Verlinde en auteur Thijs Demeulemeester voor dit boek bezochten. Met exotische objecten, avontuurlijke kleuren en persoonlijke souvenirs vertellen hun huizen de trip van hun leven.

Als corona ons één ding geleerd heeft, dan wel dit: waarom zou je je suf zoeken naar vakantieadresjes, als je thuis evengoed geïnspireerd kunt worden? Wees een indoor-nomade. Maak van je huis je favoriete reisbestemming. Zet dat maar eens op een koffiekop.

fr

« I'd rather have a passport full of stamps than a house full of stuff », entend-on parfois soupirer les globe-trotteurs dans l'âme. Jolie citation sur une tasse de café. Mais pourquoi faudrait-il choisir entre l'un ou l'autre ? Pourquoi un intérieur ne pourrait-il pas ressembler à un palpitant récit de voyage ?

Pour preuve : l'intérieur de 19 grands voyageurs, que le photographe Jan Verlinde et l'auteur Thijs Demeulemeester présentent dans cet ouvrage. Leurs maisons racontent le périple de leur vie à la lumière d'objets exotiques, de couleurs audacieuses et de souvenirs personnels.

Si la COVID-19 nous a enseigné une chose, c'est bien celle-ci : pourquoi chercher sans relâche une bonne adresse de vacances si l'on peut trouver l'inspiration chez soi ? Devenez un(e) nomade sédentaire. Faites de votre maison votre destination de voyage par excellence. Une autre maxime à placer sur votre tasse de café.

'I'd rather have a passport full of stamps than a house full of stuff,' you'll sometimes hear people with wanderlust say. Nice slogan for a coffee mug. But why not have your cake and eat it too? An interior can just as easily be an exciting travel story, can't it?

Just look at the 19 globetrotters who were visited by photographer Jan Verlinde and author Thijs Demeulemeester for this book. Filled with exotic objects, adventurous colours and personal souvenirs, their homes tell stories about the trip of a lifetime.

If there is one thing the pandemic has taught us, it's this: why spend weeks scouring websites for fun holiday destinations when you can find inspiration at home? Be an indoor nomad. Make your home your favourite travel destination. Put that on a coffee mug.

h(   )mes for nomads

Roaring seventies.

Derek Van Heurck is a *contemporary* nomad: he neither needs nor wants a dining table, and his kitchen is just a bar. This moody flat feels like a *hotel room*, where he comes and goes as he pleases.

Derek Van Heurck – creative director of fashion label Bellerose – turned a classic 1925 Art Deco flat in Brussels into a sexy apartment with a 1970s vibe. That took some radical choices. He hid the 'old-fashioned' original parquet flooring under black wall-to-wall carpet. And instead of leaving all the walls 'modernist white', he painted them a deep dark green. 'I was trying to recreate the comforting atmosphere of a pub. This is where I retreat in the winter, so I wanted something cosy. In summer I'll be sitting outside a café or by the sea anyway.' There is no dining table in Van Heurck's apartment, and his kitchen is a glossy rosewood bar. His living room looks like a hotel lobby with Camaleonda sofas placed back-to-back: one for watching TV and one for entertaining friends. Derek usually selects his interior pieces on impulse. 'Ideally, I like to mix styles, periods and origins. I buy based on love at first sight: I see something and have to have it. The only exception is the Paavo Tynell desk lamp next to the fireplace: I went out specifically looking for that one. Fortunately, I already had experience in interior design, since I've been decorating Bellerose shops for ten years by now.' www.bellerose.com

'I prefer design from the 1970s and '80s rather than the 1950s. And I like Scandinavian vintage the least, because it's fairly refined and sophisticated. I would much rather have bolder pieces from America and Brazil.'

nl

Van een klassiek Brussels art-decoappartement uit 1925 maakte Derek Van Heurck – creatief directeur van het modelabel Bellerose – een sexy flat met een seventiesvibe. Dat vergde radicale keuzes. Het 'ouderwetse' originele parket verstopte hij onder zwart kamerbreed tapijt. En in plaats van alle muren 'modernistisch wit' te laten, sausde hij ze diep donkergroen. 'Ik wou hier de gezellige sfeer van een kroeg. In de winter trek ik me hier terug, dus wilde ik iets knus. 's Zomers zit ik toch buiten op terrasjes of aan de kust.'

In Van Heurcks appartement staat geen eettafel: zijn keuken is een bar van glanzend palissanderhout. En zijn living lijkt wel een hotellobby met die Camaleonda-sofa's rug aan rug: één om tv te kijken en één om vrienden te ontvangen. Derek selecteert zijn interieurstukken vooral impulsief. 'Liefst meng ik alle stijlen, periodes en origines door elkaar. Ik koop op coup de foudre: ik zie het en ik moet het hebben. De enige uitzondering is de bureaulamp van Paavo Tynell naast de open haard: daar heb ik expliciet naar gezocht. Ervaring met interieur had ik gelukkig al: ik richt al tien jaar de Bellerose-winkels in.'

fr

Derek Van Heurck, directeur de la création de la marque Bellerose, a transformé un appartement art déco de 1925, courant à Bruxelles, en un havre sexy à l'ambiance seventies. Ce qui a exigé quelques choix radicaux. Il a intégralement camouflé le parquet original « d'antan » sous un tapis noir. Et au lieu de laisser tous les murs blancs, selon les canons du modernisme, il les a repeints dans un vert foncé profond. « Chez moi, je voulais retrouver l'ambiance chaleureuse d'un bar. En hiver, c'est ici que je me terre, donc je voulais quelque chose de douillet. En été, je suis plutôt dehors, sur une terrasse ou à la côte. »

L'appartement de Derek Van Heurck ne comporte pas de table à manger : sa cuisine se limite à un bar en palissandre brillant. Et son salon ressemble à un lobby d'hôtel, avec ses canapés Camaleonda placés dos à dos : un pour regarder la télé et un pour recevoir ses amis. Derek Van Heurck fonctionne plutôt à l'impulsivité quand il s'agit de choisir les pièces qui peuplent son intérieur. « Ce que je préfère, c'est mélanger les styles, les époques et les origines. Je fonctionne au coup de foudre : je vois un objet, et il me le faut. La seule exception est la lampe de bureau de Paavo Tynell, à côté du feu ouvert : je voulais précisément celle-là. Par chance, j'avais déjà une expérience de l'aménagement d'intérieur : j'ai aménagé les magasins Bellerose il y a dix ans de cela. »

en

The dark background in Derek Van Heurck's
apartment is the perfect canvas for vintage
furniture, art and custom-made rosewood
elements.

nl

De donkere achtergrond in Derek Van Heurcks appartement is het perfecte canvas voor vintage meubilair, kunst en maatwerk in palissanderhout.

fr

Les murs sombres de l'appartement de Derek Van Heurcks constituent le décor idéal pour son mobilier vintage, ses objets d'art et ses meubles sur mesure en palissandre.

a blend of camaleonda sofas *by mario bellini*
custom rosewood pieces black wall-to-wall carpet
dark-green painted walls

A cacophony in harmony.

Floral artist, interior designer, landscape architect, *atmosphere* creator: Frederiek Van Pamel is as *eclectic* as his home in Bruges. A unique universe somewhere between a *palazzo*, a Johannes Vermeer and Paul Smith.

'A house should feel collected, not decorated,' leading New York decorator Elsie de Wolfe once said. That is exactly what Frederiek Van Pamel has succeeded in doing. The Bruges native is a floral artist, landscape architect and interior decorator as well as a collector of well-worn art objects. Like nomads, they travel around in his tasteful home slash B&B in the heart of Bruges. 'My house is a collection of atmospheres. A cacophony, but in harmony,' Van Pamel says. He lives in a converted wing of an 18th-century physician's residence. Italian breche marble, Moroccan textiles, Indonesian doors, African statues, French antiques, Japanese high-gloss lacquer... The palette of materials is a world tour in and of itself. However exuberant or inconsistent the combination may sound, Van Pamel's interior is still coherent. 'I don't design gardens or interiors with a rigid, overall look. I'm seeking an intangible total atmosphere. The thing that binds everything together is my love of artisanal details.' www.frederiekvanpamel.be

'East and west, modern and classic, baroque or minimalist: I blend it all into my personal mix. My interior is like a good bouquet: a spontaneous creation, inconceivably unpredictable.'

fr

nl

'A house should feel collected, not decorated', zei de New Yorkse sterdecoratrice Elsie de Wolfe. Het is precies waar Frederiek Van Pamel in is geslaagd. De Bruggeling is bloemkunstenaar, tuinontwerper en interieurinrichter, maar ook verzamelaar van doorleefde kunstobjecten. Als nomaden reizen die rond in zijn stemmige woning slash B&B in hartje Brugge. 'Mijn huis is een verzameling van sferen. Een kakafonie, maar in harmonie', zegt hij.

Frederiek woont in de verbouwde zijvleugel van de achttiende-eeuwse dokterswoning. Italiaans brechemarmer, Marokkaans textiel, Indonesische deuren, Afrikaanse beelden, Frans antiek, Japans lakwerk... Het materialenpalet is een wereldreis op zich. Hoe overdadig of onsamenhangend die combinatie ook klinkt, toch is zijn interieur coherent. 'Ik ontwerp geen tuinen of interieurs in vastgeroeste *total looks*. Ik zoek naar een ongeziene totaalsfeer. Wat alles verbindt, is mijn liefde voor ambachtelijke details.'

« A house should feel collected, not decorated », a dit la fameuse décoratrice new-yorkaise Elsie de Wolfe. C'est exactement le défi que Frederiek Van Pamel a relevé avec brio. Le Brugeois est artiste floral, architecte d'intérieur et jardinier-paysagiste, mais aussi collectionneur d'objets d'art anciens. À l'instar de nomades, ils voyagent dans son agréable logement/B&B au cœur de Bruges. « Ma maison cumule différentes ambiances. Une cacophonie harmonieuse, en quelque sorte », déclare-t-il.

Frederiek Van Pamel vit dans une aile rénovée d'une maison de médecin datant du XVIIIe siècle. Marbre brèche italien, textile marocain, portes indonésiennes, images africaines, antiquités françaises, japonaiseries à la laque brillante... L'éventail des matériaux constitue un tour du monde en soi. Bien que cet amalgame semble exubérant ou discordant, son intérieur est pourtant cohérent. « Je ne conçois jamais un jardin ou un intérieur selon une image globale rebattue. Je recherche une ambiance inédite. C'est mon amour des détails artisanaux qui relie le tout. »

en

Floral artist Frederiek Van Pamel is a man of
contrasts. He blends baroque with rural and
ethnic influences in his home in Bruges: a
contemporary palazzo featuring a wealth
of different textures.

nl

fr

Bloemkunstenaar Frederiek Van Pamel is een
man van contrasten. Hij mixt barokke met
landelijke en etnische invloeden in zijn Brugse
woning: een hedendaags palazzo vol texturen.

L'artiste floral Frederiek Van Pamel est un
homme de contrastes. Dans son habitation
brugeoise, il a mélangé le baroque avec des
influences ethniques et rurales, créant
un palazzo moderne tout en textures.

a blend of   breche marble *limewash paint* glossy lacquer
moroccan zellige tiles lychee tree trunks
indonesian antiques

The Frida Kahlo of Antwerp.

Paulette Van Hacht, with her Antwerp-based interior shop *'Paulette in 't Stad'*, is a household name among aficionados of *bohemian vintage*. Her penthouse is a colouring book filled with glorious treasures.

Paulette Van Hacht is as colourful and spontaneous as the interior of her home. The Antwerp native's enthusiasm is infectious: wander around inside and you'll immediately feel like painting your house. 'A bland interior wasn't what I wanted at all', she says. With a hallway in oxblood red, an olive-green ceiling, a corridor with pink stripes and a living room in majorelle blue, she proves colours can take you on a journey without leaving your own flat. Paulette's taste is so wide-ranging she even dares to combine contemporary artworks by Shirley Villavicencio Pizango and Jef Meyer with antiques and curtains made from old Indian saris. An eye for aesthetics runs in Van Hacht's family. Her mother, Catherine De Vil, is an interior designer. After a trip around the world, Paulette opened a bohemian deco shop in Antwerp filled with exotic 'coup de coeurs' and sexy vintage styles. Mother and daughter recently started their own interior design brand, May I Come In. www.pauletteintstad.com

'I like to be inspired by old interior design magazines or by travelling. But I saw this blue in a French castle in *Haute Bohemians*, a book by Miguel Flores-Vianna. I headed to the paint shop with that photo in hand.'

fr

nl

Paulette Van Hacht is even kleurrijk en spontaan als haar interieur. Het enthousiasme van de Antwerpse werkt aanstekelijk: loop hier rond en je hebt meteen zin om je huis te schilderen. 'Een zouteloos interieur, dat wilde ik echt niet', zegt ze. Met een hal in ossenbloedrood, een plafond in olijfgroen, een gang met roze strepen en een salon in majorelleblauw bewijst ze hoe kleuren je laten reizen in je eigen appartement.

Paulettes smaak is zo breed, dat ze zelfs hedendaagse kunstwerken van Shirley Villavicencio Pizango en Jef Meyer durft te combineren met antiek en gordijnen van oude Indische sari's. Oog voor esthetiek zit Van Hacht in het bloed. Haar moeder, Catherine De Vil, is interieurarchitecte. Na een wereldreis opende Paulette in Antwerpen zelf een bohemian decowinkel vol exotische coup de coeurs en sexy vintage. Moeder en dochter startten recent een eigen interieurmerk: May I Come In.

Paulette Van Hacht est tout aussi bigarrée et spontanée que son intérieur. L'enthousiasme de l'Anversoise est contagieux: déambulez chez elle et vous aurez irrésistiblement envie de repeindre votre maison. « Je ne voudrais pas d'un intérieur sans saveur », dit-elle. Avec son hall couleur rouge sang de bœuf, son plafond vert olive, son couloir rayé de rose et son salon bleu Majorelle, Paulette Van Hacht prouve que de simples couleurs peuvent vous faire voyager dans votre propre appartement.

Ses goûts sont à ce point divers qu'elle ne craint pas d'associer les œuvres d'art contemporaines de Shirley Villavicencio Pizango et Jef Meyer avec des antiquités et des tentures taillées dans des anciens saris indiens. Son sens de l'esthétique est héréditaire ; sa mère, Catherine De Vil, est en effet architecte d'intérieur. Après avoir exploré le monde, Paulette Van Hacht a ouvert à Anvers une boutique de décoration d'inspiration bohème, remplie de coups de cœur et d'articles vintage sexy. Récemment, mère et fille ont lancé ensemble leur marque d'intérieur: May I Come In.

en

Paulette Van Hacht proves that daring colours
and eclectic deco objects can help you
transform a neutral interbellum flat into
a bohemian world tour.

nl

Paulette Van Hacht bewijst dat je met
gedurfde kleuren en eclectische deco-
objecten van een neutrale interbellumflat
een bohemien wereldreis kunt maken.

fr

Paulette Van Hacht prouve que couleurs
audacieuses et objets éclectiques peuvent
transformer un appartement neutre de l'entre-
deux-guerres en un tour du monde bohème.

a blend of curtains made from old saris *optimistic colours romantic antiques* sexy vintage

Partytecture.

Brussels native Pascaline Lefebvre spent ten years constructing fabulous party décors. Using that same *imagination*, she designed her own interior and furniture collection. Living here is a *feast* for the eyes.

The fact that Pascaline Lefebvre's home is a converted presbytery near Brussels is no longer visible to a casual observer. You can, however, still tell that she spent ten years running an agency that came up with exuberant party décors. 'As party architects, we had to reinvent ourselves time and time again, and I wanted that element of surprise in my home as well. The handles, the washbasin, the light fixtures: everything was designed as a one-off for this place,' she explains. Under the name Pascaline Lefebvre Créations, the Brussels-based designer now creates high-end furniture in materials such as wood, brass, steel, natural stone or enamel. 'I consider my furniture collection an ode to craftsmanship,' she says. So is her house. 'The terrazzo flooring wasn't made from small chips of natural stone, but from large marble fragments with a sophisticated colour palette. The herringbone parquet has been laid at straight angles. The kitchen cabinets are fronted with triangular rather than square wooden slats. I think it's interesting to always use materials in a slightly different way than we're used to. I see my house as one big laboratory for interior design experiments.' www.pascalinelefebvre.be

'Pascaline Lefebvre mixes valuable pieces with found treasures by anonymous makers. She doesn't like houses in which everything fits together perfectly, so she throws everything together in one mix & unmatch interior.'

fr

nl

Dat Pascaline Lefebvre in een verbouwde pastorij in een voorstad van Brussel woont, zou je niet meer zeggen. Dat ze tien jaar lang een bureau runde dat exuberante feestdecors bedacht, kun je wél nog merken. 'Omdat we ons als feestarchitect keer op keer moesten vernieuwen, wou ik dat verrassingseffect ook in mijn woning. De handgrepen, de wastafel, de luchters: alles is pièce unique ontworpen voor hier', vertelt ze.

Onder de naam Pascaline Lefebvre Créations ontwerpt de Brusselse nu high-end meubilair in bewerkelijke materialen zoals hout, messing, staal, natuursteen of email. 'Ik beschouw mijn meubelcollectie als een ode aan het craftmanship', zegt ze. Haar huis is dat evengoed. 'Het granito is niet gemaakt van kleine natuursteenschilfers, maar van grote marmerfragmenten in een uitgekiend kleurenpalet. Het parket in Hongaarse punt ligt in rechte hoeken. De keukenkasten zijn niet bekleed met vierkante houten latjes, maar met driehoekige. Ik vond het interessant om materialen altijd nét iets anders te gebruiken dan gewoonlijk. Ik zie mijn huis als één groot laboratorium voor interieurexperimenten.'

Impossible de deviner que Pascaline Lefebvre vit dans un ancien presbytère rénové de la périphérie bruxelloise... Mais qu'elle a géré pendant dix ans une agence créant des décors de fête exubérants, cela se remarque, par contre. « En tant que des architectes d'événements, nous devions chaque fois nous renouveler, et je voulais retrouver cet effet de surprise chez moi. Les poignées, le lavabo, les lustres : tous sont des pièces uniques, conçus spécialement pour cette maison », raconte-t-elle.

Aujourd'hui, sous le nom Pascaline Lefebvre Créations, la Bruxelloise crée des meubles haut de gamme dans des matériaux exploitables comme le bois, le laiton, l'acier, la pierre naturelle ou l'émail. « Je considère ma collection de mobilier comme une ode à l'artisanat », déclare-t-elle. Sa maison est à l'avenant. « Le granito n'est pas composé de fragments de pierre naturelle, mais de gros éclats de marbre dans une palette de couleurs assorties. Le parquet est posé en chevron, selon un plan perpendiculaire. Les armoires de cuisine sont recouvertes de lattes en bois non pas rectangulaires, mais triangulaires. Je trouve intéressant de toujours faire un usage des matériaux un peu différent de l'ordinaire. Je considère ma maison comme un grand laboratoire où mener des expériences en agencement intérieur. »

en

Furniture designer Pascaline Lefebvre was a
party architect for 10 years. You can tell by the
way she transformed a musty presbytery into
a surprising home full of unexpected nooks
and delightful custom-made details.

nl

Meubelontwerpster Pascaline Lefebvre was
10 jaar feestarchitecte. Dat merk je aan hoe
ze een muffe pastorij omvormde tot een
verrassende woning vol onverwachte hoekjes
en frisse maatwerkdetails.

fr

Pendant 10 ans, la créatrice de meubles
Pascaline Lefebvre a été un architecte
d'événements. Sa transformation d'un ancien
presbytère en une maison pleine d'inattendu
et de détails rafraîchissants en témoigne.

a blend of   terrazzo *pierre chareau* magenta
henry van de velde chinoiseries

Ceramics & match.

Danish ceramics dealer Annette Sloth lives in a 1970s flat in Brussels, surrounded by *design* and *ceramics* from around the world, ranging from *Japan* to *Sweden*.

Annette Sloth studied ceramics in Copenhagen but moved to Brussels with her then-partner. In 2000, she opened her gallery in Brussels: Puls Ceramics. For the past three years, the Danish dealer has been living in a plant-filled flat designed by modernist architect Willy Van Der Meeren (1923-2002). 'Fortunately, many of the original elements had been preserved. Unfortunately, not the kitchen or the wall cupboards. But the floors, the ceilings and the interior doors were all still there. Van Der Meeren supposedly recovered the floor from a demolished church in Bruges,' Sloth says. True to her Danish roots, her interior contains quite a lot of Scandinavian design and ceramics. Her hi-fi system is by Bang & Olufsen, the dining chairs by Yngve Ekström, the mouth-blown brutalist glassware by talented artist Morten Klitgaard and the yellow 'infinity' wall sculpture by Merete Rasmussen. However, some Belgian elements have also influenced this Brussels-based expat. Her sideboard – perfect for exhibiting ceramics – is by Alfred Hendrickx, while the ceramic skull is by Carmen Dionyse. 'And that stuffed alligator was a birthday present to myself. An ideal way to add some nuance to the interior.' www.pulsceramics.com

'On my dining table you'll find one of my favourite pieces from my private collection: amorphous ceramics by Aneta Regel, inspired by nature.'

fr

nl

Annette Sloth volgde een opleiding keramiek in Kopenhagen, maar verhuisde met haar toenmalige partner naar Brussel. In 2000 opende ze haar galerij Puls Ceramics in Brussel. Sinds drie jaar woont de Deense in een plantrijk appartement van de modernistische architect Willy Van Der Meeren (1923-2002). 'Gelukkig waren nog best veel originele elementen bewaard. De keuken of wandkasten helaas niet, wel de vloeren, de plafonds en de binnendeuren. Van Der Meeren zou de vloer uit een afbraak van een Brugse kerk hebben gerecupereerd', aldus Sloth.

Trouw aan haar Deense roots bevat haar interieur nogal wat design en keramiek uit Scandinavië. Haar hifi-installatie is van Bang & Olufsen, de eetkamerstoelen zijn van Yngve Ekström, het mondgeblazen brute glaswerk is van toptalent Morten Klitgaard en de gele 'oneindige' wandsculptuur van Merete Rasmussen. Bij deze expat in Brussel slopen echter ook wat Belgische elementen binnen. Haar buffetkast – ideaal om keramiek op te exposeren – is van Alfred Hendrickx, het keramieken doodshoofd van Carmen Dionyse. 'En die opgezette alligator was een verjaardagscadeau voor mezelf. Ideaal om het interieur wat te relativeren.'

Annette Sloth a suivi une formation en céramique à Copenhague avant d'emménager à Bruxelles avec son partenaire de l'époque. En 2000, elle a inauguré sa galerie Puls Ceramics dans la capitale belge. Depuis trois ans, la Danoise habite dans un appartement verdoyant, signé par l'architecte moderniste Willy Van Der Meeren (1923-2002). « Par chance, de nombreux éléments d'origine ont été conservés. Ce n'est malheureusement pas le cas de la cuisine ou des armoires murales, mais bien des sols, des plafonds et des portes intérieures. Van Der Meeren aurait récupéré les sols de la démolition d'une église de Bruges », précise Annette.

Fidèle à ses racines danoises, elle a disséminé dans son intérieur pas mal de pièces de design et de céramiques scandinaves. Son installation hifi est de marque Bang & Olufsen, les chaises de sa salle à manger sont de Yngve Ekström, la pièce brute en verre soufflé est l'œuvre du talentueux Morten Klitgaard et la sculpture murale jaune infini est signée Merete Rasmussen. Cependant, quelques éléments belges se sont aussi invités chez cette expatriée bruxelloise. Son buffet — parfait pour exposer des céramiques — a été réalisé par Alfred Hendrickx, et la tête de mort en céramique est de Carmen Dionyse. « Et cet alligator empaillé est un cadeau que je me suis offert pour mon anniversaire. Il relativise à merveille l'intérieur. »

a blend of   tactile ceramics *scandinavian design*
pop colours *taxidermy* plants

Kinfolk vs loft.

From sterile loft in a former *glass factory* to balanced home with *Japanese* influences. A bold facelift, designed by AE Studio.

The nomadic look of Kinfolk magazine: a style high on the wish list of the owner of this three-storey apartment in Ghent. She wanted a light, intimate cocoon where she could unwind. AE Studio translated her wish into a serene home without flashy furniture or extreme materials. 'Japanese design was one of our biggest references. The Japanese are known for their subdued aesthetics, eye for detail and love of traditional craftsmanship,' interior designer Ellen Van Laer explains. For the office and the bedroom, AE Studio designed walls resembling those of traditional Japanese ryokans – not panels of transparent rice paper, but white-painted walls with a grid of wooden slats. Another clever detail is the little glass office alcove, a retreat where the owner can meditate or read a book. Downstairs, AE Studio balanced the industrial loft feeling with warm, artisanal and eclectic touches. Like the Bulthaup kitchen, which was given a new base in herringbone parquet. Or the dining table in blackened oak, combined with weathered Gnomeman chairs: English craftsmanship with (kin)folkloric details. www.aestudio.be

'Harmony and serenity were fortunately not synonymous with a dull interior that evokes no narrative at all. AE Studio blended different storylines into a compelling travel story.'

fr

nl

De nomadische look van Kinfolk Magazine: dat stond hoog op de wishlist van de eigenares van deze Gentse flat met drie verdiepingen. Ze wou een lichte en intieme cocon om tot rust te komen. AE Studio vertaalde haar wens naar een serene woning, zonder schreeuwerige meubels of extreme materialen. 'Japans design was een van onze grootste referenties. Japanners staan bekend om hun verstilde esthetiek, oog voor detail en hun liefde voor ambacht', zegt interieurarchitecte Ellen Van Laer.

In het bureau en de slaapkamer ontwierp AE Studio wanden zoals in traditionele Japanse ryokans. Niet in transparant rijstpapier, maar met witgeschilderde muren met een rooster van houten latjes. Knap is ook het glazen bureaunisje, waar de eigenares zich kan terugtrekken om te mediteren of een boek te lezen. Beneden balanceerde AE Studio het industriële loftgevoel uit met warme, artisanale en eclectische toetsen. Zoals de Bulthaup-keuken, die een nieuwe sokkel in Hongaarsepuntparket kreeg. Of de eettafel in zwartgeblakerde eik, gecombineerd met doorleefde Gnomeman-stoelen: Engels vakwerk met (kin)folkloristische details.

Le style nomade du Kinfolk Magazine figurait en haut des désirs de la propriétaire de ce loft gantois de trois étages. Elle souhaitait un cocon épuré et intime où se reposer. AE Studio a traduit ses désirs en une habitation empreinte de sérénité, sans mobilier tape-à-l'œil ni matériaux extrêmes. « Nous nous sommes principalement inspirés du design japonais. Les Japonais sont connus pour leur esthétique équilibrée, leur souci du détail et leur amour du travail artisanal », explique l'architecte d'intérieur Ellen Van Laer.

Dans le bureau et la chambre à coucher, AE Studio a placé des cloisons pour évoquer un ryokan traditionnel japonais. Ces cloisons ne sont pas en papier de riz translucide, mais sont peintes en blanc et recouvertes d'un lattage en bois. La niche du bureau est également une excellente idée : la propriétaire peut s'y retirer pour méditer ou lire. En bas, AE Studio a atténué l'aspect industriel que dégageait le loft par des notes éclectiques chaudes et artisanales. La cuisine Bulthaup en est un exemple : le bloc de cuisine a été paré d'un parquet en chevron. La table à manger en chêne peint en noir associée à des chaises Gnomeman de deuxième main en est un autre : une fabrication anglaise présentant des détails (kin-)folkloriques.

en

AE Studio breathed new life into an industrial
triplex apartment with expressive details in
wood. In a quest for serenity, she blended lofty
elements with Japanese artisanal details.

nl

AE Studio blies een industriële triplex warmte
in met sprekende details in hout. In een
zoektocht naar sereniteit mengde ze lofty
elementen met Japanse artisanale details.

fr

AE Studio a su apporter de la chaleur à un
triplex industriel grâce à des touches de bois
expressives. Les éléments loft et des détails
artisanaux japonais s'entremêlent dans
une quête de sérénité.

a blend of   herringbone parquet *hammered glass*
gnomeman chairs japanese ryokan *piet hein eek*

Bold &
Beautiful.

'Make your home your favourite travel destination': that's the motto of Véronique Priem and Toon Stockman. Their home feels like a freaked-out *road trip* with *unexpected* pit stops.

Why spend weeks scouring websites for fun holiday destinations when you can just as easily find inspiration at home? Véronique Priem and Toon Stockman enjoy giving their house all the charm of a quirky boutique hotel. Do you know anyone else with a bedroom in green, black and purple? A desk in glossy bright red lacquer? A fireplace with navy blue and white stripes? And an open kitchen with doors covered in white skai, the retro fake leather that featured so prominently in tacky 1970s bars? Together, Véronique and Toon founded Gazeuse, a design agency that specialises in branding, packaging and communication. They recently launched their own deco line, Suchalike. The couple transformed their cottage-style home into a place that pops and that changes with the seasons. They chose colours, objects or combinations without following the rules. 'Don't be afraid to combine things. Don't waste time wondering whether something will fit in your home. Have the guts to break the so-called rules of taste,' Véronique says. 'And dare to make mistakes: nothing is forever in your interior. Changing a piece of furniture or repainting a wall is a piece of cake.' www.suchalike.com www.gazeuse.be

'When in doubt about a
purchase, always choose
the item you like best, not the
one that goes with the rest.'

nl

Waarom zou je je suf zoeken naar leuke vakantieadresjes,
als je thuis even geïnspireerd kunt raken? Véronique Priem
en Toon Stockman geven hun huis graag de allure van een
eigenzinnig boetiekhotel. Of ken jij nog veel mensen met een
slaapkamer in groen, zwart en paars? Een knalrood bureau in
hoogglanslak? Een schouw met marineblauw-witte strepen?
En een open keuken met deuren in wit skai, dat retro nepleder
dat je in tacky seventiesbars zag?

Véronique en Toon richtten samen designbureau Gazeuse
op, gespecialiseerd in branding, packaging en communicatie.
Recent lanceerden ze hun eigen decolijn, Suchalike. Het koppel
transformeerde hun huis in fermettestijl tot een knalinterieur,
dat wisselt met de seizoenen. Ze kiezen kleuren, objecten of
combinaties zonder handboek. 'Wees niet bang om zaken
te combineren. Twijfel niet of iets in je huis zal passen. Durf
de zogezegde "regels van de smaak" te overtreden', zegt
Véronique. 'En durf ook fouten te maken: niks is voor eeuwig
in je interieur. Een meubel wisselen of een muur overschilderen
is zo gebeurd.'

fr

Pourquoi chercher sans relâche une chouette adresse de
vacances si l'on peut trouver l'inspiration chez soi ? Véronique
Priem et Toon Stockman aiment donner à leur maison l'aspect
d'un hôtel-boutique hors du commun. Connaissez-vous
beaucoup de personnes dont la chambre à coucher se décline
en vert, noir et violet ? Ou qui ont un bureau rouge vif brillant ?
Une cheminée parée de rayures blanches et bleu marine ?
Une cuisine ouverte aux portes en skaï blanc, ce similicuir
rétro populaire dans les bars des années 1970 ?

Ensemble, Véronique et Tom ont fondé l'agence de design
Gazeuse, spécialisée dans l'image de marque, les emballages
et la communication. Récemment, ils ont lancé leur propre
ligne de décoration, Suchalike. Le couple a transformé sa
maison, de style fermette, en un intérieur pimpant qui change
au fil des saisons. Ils choisissent les couleurs, les objets ou
les combinaisons qui leur plaisent, sans mode d'emploi.
« N'ayez pas peur d'associer des éléments. Ne vous demandez
pas si quelque chose ira dans votre intérieur. Osez enfreindre
les "règles du bon goût", déclare Véronique. Et osez aussi
commettre des erreurs : rien ne durera des siècles dans
votre intérieur. Rien de plus simple que de remplacer un
meuble ou de repeindre un mur. »

a blend of   high-gloss lacquer *1970s skai faux leather*
funky vintage graphic prints and bold colours

New weave.

He has worked for Dries Van Noten and Jean Paul Gaultier. But *textile artist* Christoph Hefti mainly interweaves trendy flea-market finds with his own *carpet designs* in his Brussels flat.

Swiss textile artist Christoph Hefti is a fashion nomad. He has already spent half a lifetime in the international fashion world, from Paris to Zurich, London to Stockholm. Hefti has worked for big names like Jean Paul Gaultier, Dries Van Noten, Lanvin, Balenciaga and Acne Studios. In the end, however, he went his own way. A courageous gamble, though he never quite relinquished his ties to textiles and craftsmanship. Working with remnants of fabric, textile samples and thread, he now makes contemporary carpets. There's something animistic about Hefti's textile art: his colourful carpets are patchworks of fantastical creatures, myths and stories. And that is exactly how this Swiss man lives. His interior is a collage of flea-market finds, his own textile designs, colourful ceramics and fabulous vintage. It's a highly personal universe that offers a dazzling reflection of his love of colours and textures.

'I worked for Dries Van Noten for thirteen years. When he later gave me the chance to exhibit my carpets in his Los Angeles boutique, I was extremely happy. Everything came full circle.'

fr

Le designer textile et artiste suisse Christoph Hefti est un nomade de la mode. De paris à Zurich et de Londres à Stockholm : il a passé la moitié de sa vie dans le monde de la mode, sur la scène internationale. Il a notamment travaillé pour Jean-Paul Gaultier, Dries Van Noten, Lanvin, Balenciaga et Acne Studios. Après cela, il a tracé sa propre route en réalisant des tapis noués à la main, des rideaux imprimés et des lampes en céramique. Un pari courageux, même s'il n'a jamais tout à fait perdu le lien avec le textile et l'artisanat. Aujourd'hui, il crée des patchworks contemporains avec des chutes de tissus, des échantillons textiles et des fils.

L'art textile de Hefti a quelque chose d'animiste : ses tapis bariolés associent pêle-mêle créatures imaginaires, mythes et légendes. C'est du reste précisément le mode de vie de l'artiste suisse : son intérieur est un patchwork de pièces dénichées sur les marchés aux puces, de ses propres œuvres textiles, de céramiques bigarrées et d'articles vintage loufoques. Un univers extrêmement personnel, qui exprime bien son amour des couleurs et des textures.

nl

De Zwitserse textielontwerper en kunstenaar Christoph Hefti is een modenomade. Van Parijs tot Zürich, van Londen tot Stockholm: hij heeft er al een half leven in de internationale fashionwereld op zitten. Hefti werkte onder meer voor Jean Paul Gaultier, Dries Van Noten, Lanvin, Balenciaga en Acne Studios. Uiteindelijk ging hij zijn eigen weg: handgeknoopte tapijten, geprinte gordijnen en lampen in keramiek. Een moedige gok, ook al loste hij de band met textiel en craftmanship nooit echt helemaal. Met restpartijen stoffen, textielstalen en garen maakt hij nu hedendaagse patchworks.

Hefti's textielkunst heeft iets animistisch: zijn kleurrijke tapijten zijn collages van fantasiewezens, mythes en verhalen. En dat is precies hoe de Zwitser zelf woont. Zijn interieur is een assemblage van rommelmarktvondsten, eigen textielontwerpen, kleurrijke keramiek en gekke vintage. Een hoogst persoonlijk universum, waar zijn liefde voor kleuren en texturen van afspat.

a blend of   bold ceramics *ethnic carpets*
graphic prints playful vintage

Catch of the day.

Don't let the *stuffed shark* in the living area startle you: Bart Lens renovated his holiday home by the Belgian coast in a nautical theme *featuring fish and boats*.

Every detail practically shouts that architect Bart Lens had tons of fun renovating this city farm in Nieuwpoort into an 85m² holiday home. The house itself has a less light-hearted history, however: a lady who once lived here was just a baby when both her parents were killed in a bombing during WWI. Lens nicknamed this cute little terraced house on the Belgian coast 'Vis-a-vis': a multilingual pun on the fish theme that suffuses the entire interior. And he's taken it pretty far, too. From a coffee table that takes inspiration from a fish skeleton and a two-metre-long stuffed shark to a decanter shaped like a fish head: Bart Lens is not averse to a dose of flea-market kitsch in his country home. Even the custom details in his house follow the theme. Almost all the ceilings, walls, furniture and floors are made of walnut finished with boat varnish. All that polished wood conjures up the atmosphere of a luxurious cabin. And we're more than happy to come aboard. www.lensass.be

'No computers were
involved in this project.
We communicated with
the craftsmen using
sketches on paper.'

fr

nl

Aan alles merk je dat architect Bart Lens zich kostelijk heeft
geamuseerd, toen hij deze Nieuwpoortse stadsboerderij
renoveerde tot een vakantieverblijf van 85 m². Ook al kleeft
aan het huis zelf een minder amusante geschiedenis: hier
woonde ooit een dame die als baby een bombardement tijdens
de Eerste Wereldoorlog overleefde waarbij haar beide ouders
stierven.

'Vis-a-vis' is de bijnaam van Lens' schattige rijhuisje aan de
Belgische kust: een knipoog naar het vissenthema waarin het
hele interieur baadt. Dat gaat behoorlijk ver. Van een salontafel
in de vorm van een vissenskelet, een opgezette haai van twee
meter lang tot drinkkaraffen met een vissenkop: Bart Lens is in
zijn buitenverblijf niet vies van een portie rommelmarktkitsch.
Ook het maatwerk in zijn huisje pakte hij op een thematische
manier aan. Vrijwel alle plafonds, muren, meubels en vloeren
zijn uitgevoerd in notenhout, afgewerkt met bootlak. Dat geeft
het interieur de sfeer van een luxeueze kajuit. Eentje
waar we met plezier aan boord gaan.

La joie qu'a ressentie Bart Lens en rénovant sa fermette
urbaine de Nieuport en une maison de vacances de 85 m²
transpire partout. Même si l'histoire de cette fermette est
moins drôle en soi : elle fut la maison d'une femme qui a
survécu à un bombardement quand elle était bébé, lors de
la Première Guerre mondiale, tandis que ses deux parents
n'ont pas survécu.

Cette adorable maisonnette mitoyenne de la côte belge a
été surnommée « Vis-à-vis » (en néerlandais, « vis » signifie
poisson), en clin d'œil à la thématique choisie pour l'intérieur.
Cette thématique se retrouve partout : de la table de salon en
forme de squelette de poisson au requin de deux mètres de
long empaillé, en passant par les carafes à tête de poisson,
Bart Lens n'a pas peur de mettre un peu de kitsch glané sur les
brocantes dans sa maison de vacances. Même les travaux sur
mesure ont été pensés en fonction de ce thème. Pratiquement
tous les murs, plafonds, sols et meubles sont en noyer
recouvert de vernis bateaux. Ce qui confère à l'intérieur
un air de cabine de luxe. Une cabine qui donne envie
de monter à bord.

en

From bespoke work in varnished walnut to
fish-themed ceramics: Bart Lens left nothing
untouched as he created a nostalgic nautical
atmosphere for his holiday home.

nl

Van het maatwerk in geverniste notelaar tot de
keramiek in vissenthema: Bart Lens liet geen
enkel detail ongemoeid om zijn vakantiewoning
in een nostalgische bootsfeer onder te
dompelen.

fr

Des éléments en noyer vernis sur mesure aux
céramiques sur le thème marin : Bart Lens n'a
négligé aucun détail pour donner à sa maison
de vacances un air de cabine de bateau rétro.

a blend of walnut wood *nautical deco objects* muschelkalk *limestone* stuffed animals *kitsch*

Indoor mixologist.

He dreamt of a life as a *drummer*, studied film at university, but went on to become a decorator slash graphic *designer*. Brussels-born Christophe Remy is a jack-of-all-trades – something his *eclectic* flat clearly reflects.

Christophe Remy's passions range so far and wide he felt forced to stylistically split his interior. His 1928 Brussels flat is a joyride through the history of applied arts in the 20th century. He smoothly blends Art Deco with Scandinavian vintage by Pierre Forsell, a room divider by Ludvik Volak and a Sputnik chandelier. The basso continuo underlying his interior is dark green and gold: the colour combination that keeps the decorative mayonnaise from curdling. Creativity runs in Remy's blood: his grandfather was a silversmith, his great-grandfather a sculptor. You can tell from the heavy curtains, the twilight lamps and the antiques that Remy's frame of reference is classical. After his film studies, he started working with interior decorator Thierry Thenaers. During that time, he learned to compose interiors in the tradition of the grand décorateurs. In addition to being an interior designer, Remy is also a creative strategist and graphic designer – credentials evident at every turn. The original terrazzo floor of the building gave him free rein to go wild with prints and patterns of all kinds. Formal or playful, classic or modern: why choose when you can throw it all together in one big 'melting spot'? www.christopheremy.net

'The geometry and exoticism of the Art Deco period were the starting point for the interior of my flat, which dates back to 1928.'

fr

nl

Christophe Remy's passies liggen zo ver uit elkaar, dat zijn interieur stilistisch wel een grand écart moest maken. Zijn Brusselse appartement uit 1928 is een joyride door de toegepaste kunstgeschiedenis van de twintigste eeuw. Vlotjes mixt hij art deco met Scandinavische vintage van Pierre Forsell, een roomdivider van Ludvik Volak en een Sputnik-luster. De basso continuo van zijn interieur is donkergroen en goud: de kleurencombinatie waardoor de decoratieve mayonaise niet schift.

Remy heeft creativiteit in het bloed: zijn grootvader was zilversmid, zijn overgrootvader beeldhouwer. Aan de zware gordijnen, de schemerlampen en het antiek merk je dat het referentiekader van Remy klassiek is. Na zijn filmstudies kon hij aan de slag bij decorateur Thierry Thenaers. Daar leerde hij interieurs componeren in de traditie van de grand décorateurs. Naast interieurdesigner is Remy ook creatief strateeg en grafisch ontwerper. En dat kan hij niet onder designstoelen of -banken steken. De originele terrazzovloer in het flatgebouw gaf hem een vrijgeleide om los te gaan met prints en patronen allerhande. Stijf of speels, klassiek of modern: waarom kiezen als je alles kunt samengooien in één *melting spot*?

Les passions de Christophe Remy sont tellement éloignées les unes des autres que son appartement fait forcément le grand écart au niveau du style. Son appartement bruxellois datant de 1928 retrace à lui seul l'histoire des arts appliqués du 20e siècle. Il allie allègrement l'art déco à des objets vintage scandinaves de Pierre Forsell, à une cloison de séparation de Ludvik Volak et à un lustre Sputnik. La constante de son intérieur est la combinaison de couleurs vert foncé et or, qui empêche sa mayonnaise décorative de tourner.

Remy a la créativité dans le sang : son grand-père était orfèvre, son arrière-grand-père, sculpteur. On remarque aux lourdes tentures, aux antiquités et aux éclairages d'ambiance que le cadre de référence de Remy est classique. Après ses études de cinéma, il a travaillé pour le décorateur Thierry Thenaers, auprès duquel il a appris à composer des intérieurs dans la tradition des grands décorateurs. En plus de concevoir des intérieurs, Remy est aussi un stratège créatif et un concepteur graphique, et cela saute aux yeux. Le sol d'origine en terrazzo de l'appartement lui a permis d'opter librement pour des imprimés et des gabarits de toutes sortes. Sérieux ou ludique, classique ou moderne : pourquoi choisir quand on peut tout mettre dans le même *melting spot* ?

en

Creative strategist slash graphic designer
Christophe Remy lives in an apartment from
1928, but his generous interpretation of Art
Deco style expresses a period of exotic and
graphic influences.

nl

fr

Creatief strateeg en grafisch ontwerper
Christophe Remy woont wel in een
appartement uit 1928, maar hij interpreteerde
de art-decostijl heel breed als een periode
van exotische en grafische invloeden.

Bien que le stratège créatif et concepteur
graphique Christophe Remy vive dans un
appartement de 1928, sa vision du style art
déco est très large, vécue comme une série
d'influences exotiques et graphiques.

a blend of   pierre forsell design *ludvik volak* room dividers
              antiques green and gold *colourful ceramics*

Palm Springs in Belgium.

No, you won't find this elevated *circular house* in Los Angeles, but in the green belt around Antwerp. Architect Dirk Engelen has meticulously restored such homes, but did not want to *live* in a *time machine* himself.

An occupational hazard, no doubt, but Dirk Engelen, co-founder of B-architects and B-bis architects, always plans his trips around architectural highlights. The Brazilian modernism of Niemeyer and Co, the Case Study Houses in California: he can tick them all off his global 'to-see list'. Until recently, Engelen lived in a three-storey brutalist flat in Antwerp, which had a Brazilian feel. He was surprised and delighted to discover an elevated circular house in the style of the 1970s in the Belgian town of Herentals. It immediately reminded him of John Lautner's 'Elrod House' (1968) in Palm Springs. Both are built from overlapping concrete discs, and both have a circular swimming pool. The unique concept house is a masterpiece by Jackie Cuylen, a local and relatively unknown architect. A ground-floor hallway provides access to an impressive spiral staircase that leads to circular living quarters overlooking the treetops. 'We first wanted to take the time to experience the rooms and discover what we needed to restore,' Engelen explains. He did so with surgical precision: many invisible interventions made the spacious residence purer and more energy-efficient. At the same time, he furnished the James Bond-style home with contemporary artworks and vintage design. A dash of Palm Springs in Belgium. www.b-architecten.be

'I sometimes have the
bizarre feeling that this house
has been waiting for me.'

fr

nl

Beroepsmisvorming waarschijnlijk, maar Dirk Engelen, medeoprichter van B-architecten en B-bis architecten, plant zijn reizen altijd rond architecturale highlights. Het Braziliaanse modernisme van Niemeyer en co, de Case Study Houses in California: hij kan ze allemaal al afvinken van zijn mondiale to see-lijst. Zelf woonde Engelen tot voor kort in een brutalistische flat met drie verdiepingen in Antwerpen, die Braziliaans aanvoelde. Groot was zijn verbazing toen hij in Herentals een cirkelvormige paalwoning in seventiesstijl ontdekte. Die deed hem meteen aan John Lautners 'Elrod House' (1968) in Palm Springs denken. Beide zijn gebouwd uit overlappende schijven in beton. En beide hebben een rond zwembad.

De unieke conceptwoning is het meesterwerk van Jackie Cuylen, een lokale, onbekende architect. Via een gelijkvloerse sas kom je via een monumentale draaitrap in de circulaire woonvertrekken terecht. Je leeft er met je neus in de boomkruinen. 'We wilden eerst de tijd nemen om de ruimtes te beleven en te ontdekken wat we moesten restaureren', zegt Engelen. Dat deed hij met chirurgische precisie: er zijn veel onzichtbare ingrepen gebeurd die de villa zuiverder en energiezuiniger maakten. Tegelijk richtte hij de James Bondachtige woning in met hedendaagse kunstwerken en vintage design. Een vleugje Palm Springs in België.

fr

Déformation professionnelle ? Dirk Engelen, cofondateur de B-architecten et B-bis architecten, planifie toujours ses voyages autour de bijoux architecturaux. Le modernisme brésilien de Niemeyer & co, les Case Study Houses de Californie : il peut les cocher sur sa liste des choses à voir dans le monde. Jusqu'il y a peu, Dirk Engelen lui-même habitait à Anvers, dans un appartement brutaliste sur trois niveaux, à l'ambiance brésilienne. Quel ne fut pas son étonnement quand il découvrit une maison circulaire sur pilotis de style seventies à Herentals ! Elle lui évoqua tout de suite Elrod House à Palm Springs, conçue par John Lautner en 1968. Toutes deux présentent des pans de béton qui se chevauchent. Et toutes deux ont une piscine ronde.

Cette conception unique est le chef-d'œuvre de Jackie Cuylen, un architecte local méconnu. On arrive dans les pièces à vivre par un sas au rez-de-chaussée, puis un escalier en colimaçon monumental. Ici, on vit le nez dans la cime des arbres. « Nous voulions d'abord prendre le temps de connaître les lieux et de voir ce qu'il fallait restaurer », indique Dirk Engelen. Cette restauration, il l'a effectuée avec une précision chirurgicale : la villa a bénéficié d'énormément d'interventions invisibles qui la rendent plus écologique et moins énergivore. Parallèlement, il a décoré cette villa digne de James Bond avec des œuvres d'art contemporaines et des objets design. Bref, une touche de Palm Springs en Belgique.

en

Jackie Cuylen's Brutalist villa is a coherent
stack of cylinders in brick and concrete.
Architect Dirk Engelen restored them as
imperceptibly as possible, to extend their
lease on life for another 50 years.

nl

Jackie Cuylens brutalistische villa is een
consequente stapeling van cilinders in
baksteen en beton. Architect Dirk Engelen
restaureerde ze zo onzichtbaar mogelijk en
maakte ze klaar voor de volgende 50 jaar.

fr

La villa brutaliste de Jackie Cuylen
ressemble à de gros cylindres de brique et
de béton empilés. L'architecte Dirk Engelen
l'a restaurée pour les 50 ans à venir avec
discrétion et conscience écologique.

a blend of   john lautner *brutalism* ds-600 de sede
contemporary art concrete & bricks *ligne roset*

Upcycling deluxe.

With the colours of *Paul Klee*, a staircase à la *Frank Lloyd Wright* and old building materials, Joris and Caroline Van Apers created an *experimental* house full of textures.

As a specialist in old building materials, Joris Van Apers creates interiors full of expressive textures and historical references. You could hardly call it upcycling: using recycled elements, Van Apers and his wife Caroline have turned their family home into an experimental journey through centuries of art and history – without making it boring or stuffy. Parquet from Italy, red Yorkstone, slate from Portugal, Burgundian terracotta tiles… Their house is an aesthetic patchwork that still manages to look surprisingly coherent. Even their house itself is a form of recycling. In 2000, Van Apers built himself a Frank Lloyd Wright-like 'usonian house'. The more he looked for and found old building materials, the more he wanted to transform his somewhat sterile home into something more lived-in. For the pièce de résistance of the renovation – the monumental spiral staircase – he found inspiration in Frank Lloyd Wright's Guggenheim in NYC. For colours, he looked to the work of Paul Klee. 'We actually wanted to reproduce an entire painting by Klee on the walls,' says Caroline. 'But that was a bit too much.' www.vanapers.be

'The interior of our house
was a work in progress. We
often decided in the moment
which textures or materials
we wanted to add.'

fr

nl

Als specialist in oude bouwmaterialen creëert Joris Van
Apers interieurs vol sprekende texturen en historische
referenties. Upcycling kun je het nauwelijks nog noemen:
met gerecupereerde elementen maken Van Apers en zijn
vrouw Caroline van hun gezinswoning een experimentele reis
door de (kunst)geschiedenis. Zonder dat het saai of stoffig
wordt. Parket uit Italië, rode Yorkstone, leisteen uit Portugal,
Bourgondische terracottategels... Hun huis is een esthetisch
patchwork dat toch verrassend coherent oogt.

Zelfs hun huis is een vorm van recycling. In 2000 bouwde
Van Apers voor zichzelf een Frank Lloyd Wright-achtig usonian
house. Hoe meer oude bouwmaterialen hij zocht en vond,
hoe meer het kriebelde om zijn ietwat steriele woning te
transformeren naar iets doorleefds. Voor de eyecatcher van de
verbouwing – de monumentale draaitrap – vond hij inspiratie bij
Frank Lloyd Wright en zijn Guggenheim New York. En voor de
kleuren keek hij naar het werk van Paul Klee. 'Eigenlijk wilden
we een heel tafereel van Klee naschilderen op de muren',
zegt Caroline. 'Maar dat was een beetje *too much*.'

Spécialiste des matériaux de construction anciens, Joris Van
Apers imagine des intérieurs remplis de textures parlantes et
de références historiques. Cela va bien au-delà de l'upcycling:
à l'aide d'éléments récupérés, Joris et sa femme Caroline
transforment leur logement familial en un voyage expérimental
au fil de l'histoire (de l'art). Mais ce n'est ni ennuyeux ni
poussiéreux ! Du parquet italien, de la pierre rouge de York, du
schiste portugais, des carreaux en terre cuite de Bourgogne...
La maison s'apparente à un patchwork de styles qui donne
pourtant un ensemble visuel étonnamment cohérent.

La maison elle-même provient d'une sorte de recyclage :
en 2000, Joris Van Apers s'est construit une maison dans le
style usonian house de Frank Lloyd Wright. Plus il cherchait et
trouvait des vieux matériaux de construction, plus il ressentait
le besoin de faire de sa maison un peu stérile quelque chose
de plus personnel. Pour la pièce phare de la rénovation — le
monumental escalier en colimaçon — sa source d'inspiration a
été Frank Lloyd Wright et son musée Guggenheim à New York.
Du côté des couleurs, il s'est tourné vers l'œuvre de Paul Klee.
« À l'origine, notre volonté était de reproduire tout un tableau
de Klee sur les murs, explique Caroline. Mais ç'aurait été
un peu *too much*. »

en

Joris Van Apers is a specialist in old
building materials, his own home brings
together salvaged elements into a
warm and coherent collage.

nl

Joris Van Apers is een specialist in oude
bouwmaterialen die voor zijn eigen woning
op een coherente manier een collage van
gerecupereerde elementen compileerde
tot een warm geheel.

fr

Spécialiste des matériaux de construction
anciens, Joris Van Apers a réalisé, chez
lui, un assemblage cohérent d'éléments
de récupération qui donnent un résultat
chaleureux.

a blend of reclaimed wood *paul klee colours* frank lloyd wright *warm textures* contemporary craftmanship

Arts & Crafts.

For a couple of *globetrotters* from Antwerp, Philip Feyfer created a masculine penthouse resplendent with artisanal *luxury details*. A world tour of Phillip Lloyd Powell, Tom Ford and Jules Wabbes.

Philip Feyfer is an art consultant, design dealer and interior advisor who worked with Axel Vervoordt. The inhabitants of this penthouse with a roof garden, Koen Derkinderen and Bart Jordens, entrusted him with both the interior design and the artistic details. Koen and Bart's cosmopolitan taste is best reflected in the living room, which has been conceived as one big library. The dark oak cupboard showcases their travel souvenirs, books and artworks. From African bronze barter coins to contemporary ceramics by Enric Mestre, from Neolithic beaters from the Sahara to paintings by Gust Romijn, the co-founder of the ZERO movement: their collection is one big trip around the world. The dark wood of the library is echoed in their glamorous walk-in wardrobe, inspired by Tom Ford. The shiny fitted carpet and bronze cabinet details are nods to his masculine style. But the showstopper of the wardrobe has to be the low bench in walnut, attributed to American designer Phillip Lloyd Powell. George Nakashima, one of his contemporaries, was the inspiration for the American walnut finish of the kitchen cabinets. 'Their spirit of craftsmanship and love of natural materials are the common denominator throughout the penthouse.' www.pfeyfer.com

'From the Indonesian ancestral statues to the Jeanneret chair with its gorgeous patina, the Jules Wabbes desk or the handmade table in the winter garden, artisanal details are everywhere.'

nl

Philip Feyfer is tegelijk kunstconsultant, designdealer en interieuradviseur met een verleden bij Axel Vervoordt. Koen Derkinderen en Bart Jordens, de bewoners van dit penthouse met daktuin, vertrouwden hem zowel de binnenhuisarchitectuur als de kunst- en designtoetsen toe. De kosmopolitische smaak van Koen en Bart lees je nog het best af in de leefruimte, die opgevat is als één grote bibliotheek. Die kast in donker eikenhout is een etalage voor hun reissouvenirs, boeken en kunstobjecten. Van Afrikaans ruilgeld in brons naar hedendaags keramiek van Enric Mestre, van neolithische stampers uit de Sahara tot schilderijen van Gust Romijn, de medeoprichter van de ZERO-beweging: hun collectie is één grote wereldtrip.

Het donkere hout van de bibliotheek komt ook terug in hun glamoureuze inloopkast, die op Tom Ford is geïnspireerd. Het glanzende vaste tapijt en de bronzen kastdetails zijn knipogen naar zijn mannelijke stijl. Maar de showstopper in de inloopkast is toch de lage bank in notelaar, toegeschreven aan de Amerikaanse designer Phillip Lloyd Powell. Zijn tijdgenoot George Nakashima was de inspiratie voor het Amerikaanse notenhout waarin de keukenkasten zijn afgewerkt. 'Hun ambachtelijke spirit en liefde voor natuurlijke materialen zijn de rode draad doorheen heel het penthouse.'

fr

Philip Feyfer, qui a autrefois travaillé pour Axel Vervoordt, est à la fois consultant artistique, négociant d'articles design et conseiller d'intérieur. Koen Derkinderen et Bart Jordens, les habitants de ce penthouse avec jardin de toit, lui ont confié l'architecture d'intérieur et les notes artistiques et design. C'est dans le salon que l'on saisit le mieux le goût cosmopolite de Koen et Bart : il est conçu comme une vaste bibliothèque. Le meuble en chêne foncé fait étalage de leurs souvenirs de voyage, de leurs livres et autres objets d'art. De monnaies africaines en bronze à une céramique contemporaine d'Enric Mestre, en passant par des pilons néolithiques du Sahara et des tableaux de Gust Romijn, cofondateur du mouvement ZERO : leur collection constitue un voyage aux quatre coins du monde.

Le bois sombre de la bibliothèque se retrouve dans l'élégant dressing inspiré par Tom Ford. La moquette lisse ainsi que les détails en bronze des armoires sont autant de clins d'œil typiquement masculins. Cependant, la pièce centrale du dressing est le banc en noyer, attribué au designer américain Phillip Lloyd Powell. Son contemporain, George Nakashima, a inspiré le noyer d'Amérique choisi pour les finitions des armoires de cuisine. « Leur esprit artisanal et leur amour des matières naturelles constituent le fil rouge de tout le penthouse. »

a blend of   tom ford *travel souvenirs* george nakashima
american walnut *artisanal details*

In Lofty Praise of Folly.

Challenge Jean-Philippe Demeyer to design an *epic penthouse*, and this is the result: a festive lasagne of textures, colours and prints. An unparalleled *Gesamtkunstwerk* that dazzles the senses.

The Gesamtkunstwerk could be considered the 'full-body massage' of interior design: the interior is a comprehensive concept without any hierarchy of prominence. Every square centimetre has been carefully crafted. This penthouse in Ghent is one such complete work of art, designed by Jean-Philippe Demeyer. For a young couple, he pulled out all the decorative stops. The result: a flamboyant ode to chutzpah, playfulness and imagination. The burnt-wood ceiling and terracotta floor tiles are the only constants in this amusement park of ideas. Tiger-print carpet and mirrored doors in the hallway, cork in the bathroom, reclaimed ceramic tiles in the kitchen, an orange pantry, an 'Arcadia' tapestry in the lounge: there's a surprise around every corner. Perfect for the preferences expressed by the owners, a couple of globetrotters who enjoy exciting interiors in hotels or restaurants. But don't call their penthouse eclectic, because Demeyer doesn't like the term. 'Eclectic is synonymous with choice overload: for people who are afraid to make bold choices in their interior. I'm just very decisive in my selections, because every project has its own unique storyline.' www.jpdemeyer.com

'Eclectic is synonymous with choice overload: for people who are afraid to make bold choices in their interior. I'm just very decisive in my selections.'

fr

nl

Het gesamtkunstwerk is de full body massage van de binnenhuisarchitectuur: het interieur is een totaalconcept, waarbij hoofd- en bijzaak niet bestaan. Over elke vierkante centimeter is nagedacht. Dit penthouse in Gent is zo'n episch gesamtkunstwerk, ontworpen door Jean-Philippe Demeyer. Voor een jong koppel trok hij alle decoratieve registers open. Het resultaat: een flamboyante ode aan lef, speelsheid en verbeelding.

Het plafond in gebrand hout en de vloer in terracotta tegels zijn nog de enige constante in dit pretpark van ideeën. Vast tapijt in tijgerprint én spiegeldeuren in de hal, kurk in de badkamer, gerecupereerde keramiektegels in de keuken, een oranje voorraadkast, een 'Arcadia' wandtapijt in de salon: achter elke hoek schuilt een verrassing. Precies de wens van de eigenaars, een koppel globetrotters die houden van spannende interieurs van hotels of restaurants. Maar noem hun penthouse vooral niet eclectisch, want Demeyer houdt niet van die term. 'Eclectisch is synoniem voor keuzestress: voor mensen die niet durven te kiezen in hun interieur. Ik ben net heel beslist in mijn keuzes, want elk project heeft zijn eigen unieke verhaallijn.'

Le concept d'origine allemande de gesamtkunstwerk (œuvre d'art totale) est l'architecture d'intérieur prise comme concept global ; l'intérieur y est conçu comme un tout, sans éléments principaux ou secondaires. Chaque centimètre carré est réfléchi avec soin. Situé à Gand, ce penthouse est l'une de ces œuvres d'art totales, sorties de l'imagination de Jean-Philippe Demeyer. Il a donné libre cours à tous les registres de la décoration pour un jeune couple. Résultat : une ode flamboyante au culot, à la frivolité et à l'imagination.

Le plafond en bois brûlé et le sol recouvert de carrelage en terre cuite sont les seules constantes de ce fantastique laboratoire d'idées. Moquette tigrée et portes à miroir dans le hall, liège dans la salle de bains, carreaux de céramique de récupération dans la cuisine, placard orange, tapisserie murale « Arcadia » dans le salon : chaque recoin recèle une surprise. C'est exactement ce que souhaitaient les propriétaires, un couple de globe-trotters fans des intérieurs grandioses des hôtels et restaurants. Mais ne qualifiez surtout pas leur penthouse d'éclectique, car Demeyer n'apprécie guère ce terme. « L'éclectisme est synonyme d'embarras du choix : c'est pour les gens qui n'osent pas prendre des décisions pour leur intérieur. Or, je suis très résolu dans mes choix, car chaque projet a sa propre ligne de conduite unique. »

en

When Jean-Philippe Demeyer pulls out all
the stops, this is what you get: a cinematic
penthouse in which every room has its own
storyline – even the hallway and the bathroom.

nl

Als je Jean-Philippe Demeyer alle registers laat opentrekken, dan krijg je dit: een filmisch penthouse waar elke ruimte haar eigen verhaallijn heeft. Zelfs de gang en het toilet.

fr

Voilà ce que l'on obtient quand on donne carte blanche à Jean-Philippe Demeyer : un penthouse fantasque, où chaque espace suit sa propre thématique. Même le couloir et les toilettes.

a blend of   burnt wood *belgian terracotta tiles* cork *arcadia*
                    wall tapestry bright orange and pale yellow

Bohemian Rocksody.

If an interior is a *self-portrait*, then the house where Aline Walther and Keith Hioco live tells a story of distant *travels*, *vintage finds* and a *rock & roll life*.

Aline Walther and Keith Hioco are the designers behind the denim labels Eat Dust and Girls of Dust, adored by rock gods such as Josh Homme and Jesse Hughs. They live in Antwerp, in a 1960s newsagent and barber shop they opened up into a rock & roll loft. 'We stripped away the ugly renovations until we got down to the brutalist shell,' Aline says. Under the linoleum floor they found a cement screed, which they polished and varnished with graffiti gloss. Over time, vintage furniture, flea-market finds, plants and souvenirs from their many travels found a way into their home. 'As soon as we had some money, we upgraded our interior. It's still in transformation,' Aline adds. 'Crazy ceramics, weird stuff from Japan, heirlooms by Raf Simons: we have all sorts of things here. Our interior was collected over the years rather than bought all at once. The house pretty much tells the story of our lives,' she says. That life was already packed to the brim: Keith and Aline worked for Raf Simons, Essentiel, Bruno Pieters, Veronique Leroy and Calvin Klein before venturing into denim and setting up their own labels. 'Our interior doesn't change every season, like the latest fashions. If yellow plastic is suddenly à la mode, this place won't instantly be filled with it. I do put out some darker sheepskins in winter, though.' www.eatdustclothing.com

SCARPA

barbican ODROTHEA POLITICS PROSTEL
                LANGÉ

Gerrit Rietveld

eenvoud

wealth

Léon Stynen   1899
               1990

Léon Stynen   A Life of Architecture
               1899 1990

Jenny Saville

GAGOSIAN

'This interior was collected over the years rather than bought all at once. Our house pretty much tells the story of our lives.'

fr

nl

Aline Walther en Keith Hioco zijn de designers achter de denimlabels Eat Dust en Girls of Dust, waarvan rockgoden als Josh Homme en Jesse Hughs fan zijn. Ze wonen in Antwerpen in een sixties krantenwinkel en kapperszaak, die ze opengooiden tot rock-'n'-rollloft. 'De lelijke verbouwingen stripten we, tot we op de brute schil uitkwamen', zegt Aline. Onder het linoleum troffen ze een cementdekvloer aan, die ze polierden en vernisten met graffitilak. Mettertijd vulde het interieur zich met vintage meubilair, rommelmarktvondsten, planten en souvenirs van hun vele reizen. 'Zodra we wat geld hadden, deden we een upgrade van ons interieur. Het is nog steeds in transformatie', zegt Aline.

'Gek keramiek, weirde spullen uit Japan, erfstukken van Raf Simons: er staat hier echt van alles. Ons interieur is niet in één keer gekocht, maar bij elkaar gesprokkeld met de jaren. Het huis vertelt zo'n beetje het parcours van ons leven', zegt ze. Dat leven was al behoorlijk rijk gevuld: Keith en Aline werkten al voor Raf Simons, Essentiel, Bruno Pieters, Veronique Leroy en Calvin Klein, voordat ze zich op hun denimlabels stortten. 'Ons interieur verandert niet elk seizoen, zoals de mode. Als geel plastic plots in de mode is, zal het hier niet meteen vol staan. Maar in de winter leg ik wel wat meer donkere schapenvelletjes.'

Aline Walther et Keith Hioco sont les designers qui se cachent derrière les marques de denim Eat Dust et Girls of Dust, que des stars du rock comme Josh Homme et Jesse Hughs adorent. Ils vivent à Anvers, dans une librairie-salon de coiffure des années 1960 qu'ils ont transformée en un loft rock'n'roll. « Nous avons arraché toutes les couches d'affreuses transformations jusqu'à arriver à la coquille brute », se souvient Aline. Sous le linoléum, ils ont découvert une chape en ciment qu'ils ont lissée et recouverte de peinture pour graffiti. Au fil du temps, ils ont rempli l'intérieur de mobilier vintage, d'objets dénichés dans des brocantes, de plantes et de souvenirs de leurs nombreux voyages. « Dès que nous avions un peu d'argent, nous l'injections dans notre intérieur. C'est d'ailleurs toujours un chantier en cours », poursuit Aline.

« Des céramiques loufoques, des objets bizarres du Japon, des œuvres de Raf Simons : on trouve de tout ici. Notre intérieur n'a pas été aménagé en une fois, mais s'est constitué au fil des ans. Notre maison raconte un peu le parcours de notre vie », conclut-elle. Cette vie, elle a déjà été bien remplie : Keith et Aline ont travaillé pour Raf Simons, Essentiel, Bruno Pieters, Veronique Leroy et Calvin Klein, avant de lancer leurs propres marques de denim. « Contrairement à la mode, notre intérieur ne change pas chaque saison. Si le plastique jaune devient soudain à la mode, nous n'en intégrerons pas forcément chez nous. Cependant, en hiver, il est vrai que j'étale ici et là des peaux de mouton plus sombres. »

en

From 1960s newsagents shop to an open loft packed
with cool details: fashion couple Aline Walther and
Keith Hioco decorated their home with souvenirs
and furniture that tell their life story.

nl

Van sixtieskrantenzaak tot open loft vol stoere
details: het modekoppel Aline Walther en Keith
Hioco kleedden hun woning aan met souvenirs
en meubels die hun levensverhaal vertellen.

fr

D'une librairie des années soixante à un loft
ouvert et rock'n'roll : les stylistes Aline Walther
et Keith Hioco ont habillé leur maison de
souvenirs et de meubles qui racontent leur vie.

a blend of   vintage furniture *exotic souvenirs* reclaimed wood *plants* weathered leather

Antique, c'est chique.

Anyone who thinks *antiques* are old-fashioned has clearly never seen Sophie Helsmoortel at work. She combines vintage design, *heirlooms* and antiques in the most *glamorous* way.

Sophie Helsmoortel is the inspiring force behind the Brussels fashion boutique Cachemire coton soie. In her flat in Ixelles, she defiantly refuses to slavishly follow fashion trends. Her feel for textiles, colour, textures and materials is immediately apparent. Much like her love of Italian design: she collects Murano glass and owns lamps by Gino Sarfati and Angelo Lelli. For Helsmoortel, the challenge is to combine vintage design with antiques in fresh ways. She has succeeded handsomely with her wall of Villeroy & Boch plates, inherited from her great-grandmother. The painting in the salon is another family gem, a portrait of her mother and Sofie as a baby, painted in 1958. The true showstopper of the flat is a wall covered in sheet copper, patiently installed by a student of the renowned Institut Supérieur de Peinture Van Der Kelen-Logelain. The same touch of glamour is reflected in other design elements, such as Pierre Forsell's slender wall candle holders or the 1970s sideboard. 'To match my antique table with the décor, I specifically painted it grey and gold,' Helsmoortel says. 'I didn't paint my hallway wardrobe myself; I had it done in a jungle theme by French artist Julien Colombier. It took him more than a week.' www.cachemirecotonsoie.com

'The stuffed birds and porcelain parrots refer to the rose-ringed parakeets that fly around the parks in Brussels.'

fr

nl

Sophie Helsmoortel is de bezielster achter de Brusselse modeboetiek Cachemire coton soie. In haar appartement in Elsene volgt ze allerminst slaafs de modetrends. Haar gevoel voor textiel, kleur, textuur en materialen valt meteen op. Net als haar liefde voor Italiaans design: ze verzamelt Murano-glas en heeft lampen van Gino Sarfati en Angelo Lelli. Voor Helsmoortel is het een uitdaging om vintage design op een frisse manier te combineren met antiek. En dat is haar knap gelukt met haar wand vol borden van Villeroy & Boch, geërfd van haar overgrootmoeder. Ook het schilderij in de salon is een familiejuweel, een portret van haar moeder en Sofie als baby, geschilderd in 1958.

Dé showstopper van het appartement blijft de wand in bladkoper, geduldig uitgevoerd door een studente van het befaamde Institut Supérieur de Peinture Van Der Kelen-Logelain. Dat tikje glamour komt ook terug in andere designstukken, zoals de slanke wandkaarsenhouders van Pierre Forsell of de seventies buffetkast. 'Om mijn antieke tafel te doen matchen met het decor, heb ik ze speciaal grijs en goud geschilderd', vertelt ze. 'Mijn vestiairekast in de gang heb ik niet zelf geschilderd. Dat heeft de Franse kunstenaar Julien Colombier gedaan in junglethema. Meer dan een week was hij ermee bezig.'

Sophie Helsmoortel est la femme qui se cache derrière la boutique bruxelloise de prêt-à-porter Cachemire Coton Soie. Son appartement d'Ixelles se défie des tendances de la mode. Son sens des textiles, des couleurs, des textures et des matières se ressent tout de suite, tout comme son amour du design italien : elle collectionne les verres de Murano et possède des lampes de Gino Sarfati et d'Angelo Lelli. Pour Sophie Helsmoortel, combiner de manière esthétique vintage et antiquités constitue un défi. Défi qu'elle a magnifiquement relevé avec son mur couvert d'assiettes Villeroy & Boch héritées de son arrière-grand-mère. Le tableau du salon est lui aussi un héritage familial : un portrait de sa mère et d'elle-même bébé, peint en 1958.

Cependant, la pièce maîtresse de l'appartement est sans nul doute le mur en feuille de cuivre, patiemment réalisé par une étudiante du renommé Institut Supérieur de Peinture Van Der Kelen-Logelain. Cette note glamour se retrouve aussi dans d'autres pièces design comme les fins chandeliers muraux de Pierre Forsell ou le buffet des années 1970. « Pour que ma table, une pièce d'antiquité, cadre avec le décor, je l'ai repeinte en gris et or, commente-t-elle. Je n'ai pas peint moi-même la penderie dans le couloir. J'ai confié cette tâche, sur le thème de la jungle, à l'artiste français Julien Colombier. Cela lui a pris plus d'une semaine. »

en

Sophie Helsmoortel's apartment is full of
picturesque details. Julien Colombier dropped
by to paint the wardrobe in a jungle theme. The
painting in the living room portrays Sophie and
her mother.

nl

Sophie Helsmoortels appartement zit vol
schilderachtige details. Julien Colombier kwam
de vestiairekast beschilderen in junglethema.
Het portret in de living stelt Sophie en haar
mama voor.

fr

L'appartement de Sophie Helsmoortels
regorge de détails insolites ; Julien Colombier
a peint la penderie sur le thème de la jungle, et
le tableau dans le salon représente Sophie
et sa maman.

a blend of   gold *antiques* italian vintage design *hollywood* regency *villeroy & boch plates* julien colombier

The old house and the sea.

Why travel around the world when you could integrate all those *influences* in your *farmhouse* by the sea? Kim Verbist is living proof that a staycation can still feel *cosmopolitan*.

An Uzbek suzani quilt, fabrics from Rajasthan, an amateur painting from Hastings, kilims from Morocco: with all these souvenirs, you could easily invent a travel story based on Kim Verbist's house in Zeeuws-Vlaanderen. The real story? The Brussels-based interior designer used to be a globetrotter who designed hotel interiors across the world for major chains like Marriott, Sophos Hotels and Wyndham. Until she fell in love with a little farmhouse in Cadzand, a village by the sea in the Netherlands. She turned her world upside down: Verbist's apartment in Brussels became her pied à terre, while her farmstead in Zeeland was upgraded to her base of operations. She quickly felt at home in it. Her green thumb even got a great workout: after transforming the house, Verbist also dug deep into the garden surrounding the farm. Along a path of seashells, she created a lush flower garden that seamlessly blends into the polder landscape. You'd be willing to go on holiday in your own home with less than this. www.kim-verbist.com

'Kim Verbist worked in hotels all over the world, until she fell in love with a farmstead in Zeeuws-Vlaanderen. That kicked off her new life.'

fr

nl

Een Oezbeekse suzani-sprei, stoffen uit Rajasthan, een amateurschilderij uit Hastings, kelims uit Marokko: met al die souvenirs zou je gemakkelijk een reisverhaal kunnen bedenken aan de hand van Kim Verbists huis in Zeeuws-Vlaanderen. Het echte verhaal? De Brusselse interieurarchitecte was een globetrotter die wereldwijd hotelinrichtingen bedacht voor onder meer Mariott, Sophos Hotels en Wyndham. Tot ze verliefd werd op een boerderijtje in Cadzand, aan de Nederlandse kust.

Het is de wereld op zijn kop: Kims flat in Brussel werd haar buitenverblijf, haar hoeve in Zeeland haar uitvalsbasis. Ze voelde zich er snel thuis. En zelfs haar groene vingers begonnen te jeuken, want na haar woning pakte ze ook de tuin rond de boerderij grondig aan. Langs een pad met schelpen creëerde ze een weelderige bloementuin, die naadloos overgaat in het polderlandschap. Je zou voor minder op vakantie willen in je eigen huis.

Un jeté de lit en suzani ouzbek, des étoffes du Rajasthan, une toile amateur de Hastings, des tapis kilim marocains : il serait facile d'imaginer un récit de voyage sur la base de tous ces souvenirs rassemblés dans la maison de Kim Verbist, en Flandre zélandaise. La vérité ? L'architecte d'intérieur bruxelloise a été globe-trotteuse et a conçu l'aménagement d'hôtels un peu partout dans le monde, notamment pour les chaînes Mariott, Sophos Hotels et Wyndham. Jusqu'à ce qu'elle tombe amoureuse d'une fermette à Cadzand, sur la côte néerlandaise.

C'est le monde à l'envers : l'appartement bruxellois de Kim Verbist est devenu sa résidence secondaire, sa ferme de Zélande son port d'attache. Elle s'y est très vite sentie chez elle. Même sa main verte s'est mise à la démanger, car après avoir transformé le corps de logis, elle s'est attaquée au jardin autour de la ferme. Elle a créé un luxuriant jardin fleuri le long d'un sentier fait de coquillages, qui se perd en douceur dans les polders. On passerait ses vacances chez soi pour moins que ça...

en

Kim Verbist has designed several international
hotels. Her impressively accumulated air miles
and cosmopolitan taste can immediately be
felt in her converted little farmhouse
in Cadzand.

nl

Kim Verbist ontwierp verschillende
internationale hotels. Haar vele airmiles en
kosmopolitische smaak voel je meteen in
haar verbouwde boerderijtje in Cadzand.

fr

Kim Verbist a aménagé des hôtels pour
différentes chaînes internationales. Ses
nombreux voyages et son goût cosmopolite
se ressentent tout de suite dans sa fermette
rénovée de Cadzand.

a blend of   quirky travel souvenirs *folk art*
unpretentious vintage design *cork*

Like Mike.

Their keen eye for *quality* is a constant, but their collection of Italian, Belgian and European *design* is forever *evolving*. Welcome to the converted physician's residence design dealers Anna Battistini and Mike Standaert call their *home*.

As the scion of an Italian antique dealer's family, Anna Battistini doesn't need any lessons in recognising quality. Her husband, Mike Standaert, is a Belgian vintage-design dealer with a solid international reputation in his own right. The couple each run their own design shop, in Deurle and Ostend respectively, but also provide bespoke total interiors. Together with their two children, they live in a converted and extended physician's residence from 1920. On the outside, it fits in nicely with the picturesque artists' enclave of Deurle. Inside, however, their house frames an ever-changing collage of their cosmopolitan tastes. Fontanarte, Claudio Brocchini, Gio Ponti, Ettore Sottsass and Bruno Gambone versus Jules Wabbes, Maarten Van Severen, Jos Devriendt and Renaat Braem: the interior of Mike and Anna's home is an international match between Italy and Belgium, with vintage pieces from other European countries as the spectators. 'As design dealers, we're used to frequently changing our furnishings. Much like nomads, we don't get attached to things.' www.whiteinteriors.be   www.whiteinteriors49.be

'As design dealers, we're used to frequently changing our furnishings. Much like nomads, we don't get attached to things.'

fr

nl

Als telg uit een Italiaanse antiquairsfamilie moet je Anna Battistini niet leren wat kwaliteit is. Haar man, Mike Standaert, is een Belgische vintagedesignhandelaar van internationale faam. Het koppel runt elk een designzaak in Deurle en Oostende, al doen ze samen ook op maat gemaakte totaalinrichtingen. Samen met hun twee kinderen wonen ze in een verbouwde én uitgebreide dokterswoning uit 1920. Aan de buitenkant matcht die mooi met het pittoreske kunstenaarsdorp Deurle. Vanbinnen is hun huis echter een wissellijst voor hun wereldse smaak.

Fontanarte, Claudio Brocchini, Gio Ponti, Ettore Sottsass en Bruno Gambone versus Jules Wabbes, Maarten Van Severen, Jos Devriendt en Renaat Braem: het interieur van Mike en Anna is een interland Italië-België, gekruid met andere Europese vintage. 'Als designhandelaars zijn we gewend dat onze inrichting vaak verandert. Zoals nomaden hechten we ons niet zozeer aan spullen.'

Pas besoin d'expliquer à Anna Battistini, issue d'une famille d'antiquaires italienne, ce qu'est la qualité. Quant à son compagnon, Mike Standaert, c'est un négociant en design belge de réputation internationale. Bien que chacun gère sa propre affaire design, respectivement à Deurle et Ostende, respectivement, ils réalisent également ensemble des aménagements globaux personnalisés. Leurs deux enfants et eux-mêmes habitent une maison de médecin de 1920 rénovée et agrandie. Vue de l'extérieur, celle-ci cadre parfaitement avec le pittoresque village d'artistes de Deurle. À l'intérieur, leur habitation traduit plutôt l'éclectisme de leurs goûts.

Fontanarte, Claudio Brocchini, Gio Ponti, Ettore Sottsass et Bruno Gambone d'un côté, Jules Wabbes, Maarten Van Severen, Jos Devriendt et Renaat Braem de l'autre : leur intérieur ressemble à un match Belgique-Italie, pimenté d'autres objets vintage d'Europe. « En tant que marchands design, nous sommes habitués à ce que notre intérieur change régulièrement. À l'instar de nomades, nous ne sommes guère attachés aux objets. »

en

The interior of design dealers Mike Standaert
and Anna Battistini is a vintage voyage through
Europe, with Italian and Belgian design as the
basso continuo.

nl

Het interieur van designhandelaars Mike
Standaert en Anna Battistini is een vintagereis
door Europa. Met Italiaans en Belgisch design
als basso continuo.

fr

L'intérieur des marchands de design Mike
Standaert et Anna Battistini ressemble à une
traversée vintage de l'Europe, avec pour fil
rouge des pièces de design belge et italien.

a blend of   gio ponti *maarten van severen* jozef mees *ettore sottsass* modern design *contemporary craftmanship*

Traveller chic.

Inspired by David Hicks and Cecil Beaton, Geoffroy Van Hulle crafts interiors for *intuitive* houses that invite you to go on a *mental journey*. His eclectic studio flat in Maldegem sets the tone.

Inspired by Antoine Bourdelle's Parisian studio flat, decorator Geoffroy Van Hulle recently renovated his home together with architect Stephane Boens. His art studio has now become a canvas for his eclectic collection. Like a true bohemian, Van Hulle's inspiration comes from the four corners of the world. With great bravura, he blends all those exotic influences into a maximalist fusion style that still feels very natural. 'My big heroes are British decorator David Hicks and Cecil Beaton,' he says. 'Beaton was creative in all areas: he designed opera costumes and film sets, was a top photographer and painter, and designed interiors for jetsetters.' Geoffroy Van Hulle is self-taught. Purely by intuition, he composes his interiors as landscapes where colours, textures, volumes and objects are in balance. 'I love it when every room has a different atmosphere. You have to be able to travel in your own home,' he says. Moving on from the 'Bourdelle' living studio, his home brings you to a winter salon conceived as a Moroccan tent, a Jean Michel Frank-inspired dining room, an apartment in Yves Saint Laurent style, a 1970s winter garden and a Chinese dining room with murals by Pablo Piatti. 'I take pleasure from trying new combinations. My house is my personal playground,' he says. www.geoffroyvanhulle.com

'Every house deserves a winter and summer coat. If you change the curtains or the sofa every season, you immediately get a completely different atmosphere. You wouldn't wear the same jacket in February as in August, would you?'

fr

nl

Geïnspireerd op de Parijse atelierwoning van Antoine Bourdelle verbouwde decorateur Geoffroy Van Hulle recent zijn woning samen met architect Stephane Boens. Zijn 'kunstenaarsatelier' is nu een canvas voor zijn eclectische verzameling interieurobjecten. Als bij een echte bohemien komt inspiratie bij Van Hulle uit de vier windstreken aanwaaien. Met veel bravoure blendt hij al die exotische invloeden tot een maximalistische fusionstijl, die toch heel naturel aanvoelt. 'De Britse decorateur David Hicks en Cecil Beaton zijn mijn grote helden', zegt hij. 'Beaton was creatief op alle vlakken: hij ontwierp operakostuums en filmsets, was topfotograaf, schilder, en richtte interieurs in voor jetsetters.'

Geoffroy Van Hulle is een autodidact. Puur op intuïtie componeert hij zijn interieurs als een landschap waar kleuren, texturen, volumes en objecten in balans zijn. 'Ik hou ervan als elke kamer een andere sfeer uitstraalt. In je huis moet je op reis kunnen gaan', zegt hij. Vanuit het 'Bourdelle' woonatelier kom je bij hem terecht in een wintersalon opgevat als Marokkaanse tent, een Jean Michel Frank geïnspireerde eetkamer, een appartement in Yves Saint Laurent-sfeer, een seventies wintertuin en een Chinese eetkamer met muurschilderingen van Pablo Piatti. 'Ik amuseer me door nieuwe combinaties uit te proberen. Mijn huis is mijn speeltuin', zegt hij.

S'inspirant de la maison-atelier parisienne d'Antoine Bourdelle, le décorateur Geoffroy Van Hulle a récemment rénové sa résidence avec l'aide de l'architecte Stephane Boens. Son « atelier d'artiste » est à présent l'écrin qui abrite sa collection éclectique d'objets d'intérieur. Geoffroy Van Hulle tire son inspiration du monde entier, comme le veut le style bohème. Il mélange hardiment toutes ces influences exotiques en une fusion maximaliste, mais qui semble pourtant parfaitement naturelle. « Les décorateurs britanniques David Hicks et Cecil Beaton sont mes héros », commente-t-il. « Beaton était un créatif tous azimuts : il créait des costumes d'opéra et des décors de film, était un photographe hors pair, un peintre, et aménageait des intérieurs pour la jet-set. »

Geoffroy Van Hulle est un autodidacte. Il compose ses intérieurs, de manière purement intuitive, comme un paysage, intégrant harmonieusement couleurs, textures, volumes et objets. « J'aime que chaque pièce dégage une atmosphère différente. Il faut pouvoir partir en voyage chez soi », déclare-t-il. En sortant de sa maison-atelier de style Bourdelle, on débouche successivement dans un salon d'hiver conçu comme une tente marocaine, une salle à manger dans l'esprit de Jean Michel Frank, un appartement d'esprit Yves Saint Laurent, un jardin d'hiver des seventies puis une salle à manger chinoise avec des peintures murales de Pablo Piatti. « Cela m'amuse d'essayer de nouvelles combinaisons. Ma maison est ma salle de jeux », conclut-il.

en

'I love it when every room has a different
atmosphere. You have to be able to travel in
your own home,' says decorator Geoffroy Van
Hulle, who views his home as an artist's atelier
in which he can experiment.

nl

'Ik hou ervan als elke kamer een andere sfeer
uitstraalt. In je huis moet je op reis kunnen
gaan', zegt decorateur Geoffroy Van Hulle,
die zijn woning opvatte als een atelier
d'artiste om te experimenteren.

fr

« J'aime que chaque pièce dégage une
atmosphère différente. Il faut pouvoir voyager
chez soi », dit le décorateur Geoffroy Van Hulle.
Sa maison est comme un atelier d'artiste où
il peut créer des ambiances.

a blend of antoine bourdelle *antiques* yves saint laurent
bohemian chic cecil beaton

on contemporary nomadism

'A house should feel collected, not decorated,' Elsie de Wolfe, the first American star decorator, once said. In the 16th and 17th centuries, people with power and taste were already aware of this. They crafted Wunderkammern for themselves: a summary of the world's wonders, all packed into one room. In this 'theatre of the world' or theatrum mundi, the most wondrous objects were put on display: from stuffed animals to seashells, scientific instruments to exotic works of art. The real diehards brought their own finds home from distant countries. But most bought items from dealers, purely to impress their visitors. A cabinet of curiosities could be used to gauge a person's view of the world. It was a status symbol for people with knowledge, power, money and cosmopolitan taste. Essentially, not much has changed since then. You can still tell from an interior whether someone is highly knowledgeable or an extensive traveller – or at least likes to pretend that they are. We still bring back travel souvenirs in our urge to seek out exotic elements... or in an attempt to cling to an emotion associated with something firmly in the past. In the interiors we selected for this book, the collected objects have travelled many leagues from their original locales. Their inhabitants are modern-day nomads, whose lives no longer fit into a suitcase or a Wunderkammer. Their homes have become unique destinations that invite your mind on a journey. Photographer Jan Verlinde and author Thijs Demeulemeester are your tour guides. Enjoy the trip!

h(   )mes for nomads

nl

'A house should feel collected, not decorated',
zei Elsie de Wolfe, de eerste Amerikaanse
sterdecoratrice. In de zestiende en zeventiende
eeuw wisten ze dat ook al. Al wie macht en
smaak had, richtte toen een 'wunderkammer' in:
een samenvatting van de wereld, gebald in één
kamer. In dat 'Theatrum mundi' bundelde men de
wonderlijkste objecten: van opgezette dieren tot
schelpen, van meetinstrumenten tot exotische
kunstwerkjes. Diehards brachten die zelf mee
uit verre landen. Maar de meesten kochten die
voorwerpen bij handelaren, puur om indruk te
maken op hun bezoek. Aan de wunderkammer
kon je iemands wereldbeeld aflezen. Het was een
statussymbool van iemand met kennis, macht,
geld én kosmopolitische smaak. Eigenlijk is er
niet zoveel veranderd. Aan een interieur kun je
nog steeds afleiden of iemand veel weet of veel
reist. Of toch tenminste graag wil doen alsof.
Nog steeds brengen we reissouvenirs mee, in
een drang naar exotiek. Of in een poging om een
emotie vast te houden van iets wat definitief
voorbij is. In de interieurs die we voor dit boek
selecteerden, hebben de verzamelde objecten al
behoorlijk wat airmiles op de teller. Hun bewoners
zijn hedendaagse nomaden, wier leven al lang
niet meer in een koffer of in een wunderkammer
past. Hun woningen zijn een unieke bestemming
geworden waar je mentaal op reis kunt.
Met fotograaf Jan Verlinde en auteur Thijs
Demeulemeester als reisleiders. Enjoy the trip.

fr

Comme l'a dit Elsie de Wolfe, la première grande
décoratrice américaine : « A house should feel
collected, not decorated ». Cela se savait déjà
aux XVIe et XVIIe siècles. À l'époque, qui avait
du pouvoir et du goût possédait un « cabinet
de curiosités » où étaient rassemblées des
pièces venant du monde entier. Ce Theatrum
mundi présentait les objets les plus bizarres
; des animaux empaillés aux coquillages, en
passant par des instruments de mesure et des
objets d'art exotiques. Les irréductibles les
ramenaient eux-mêmes de contrées lointaines,
mais la plupart de ces objets étaient achetés
auprès de négociants et avaient pour seul but
d'impressionner les visiteurs. Le cabinet de
curiosités permettait de percevoir la conception
du monde de son propriétaire. C'était un symbole
de statut pour une personne lettrée, puissante,
nantie et aux goûts cosmopolites. À vrai dire,
cela n'a pas tellement changé. L'intérieur d'une
personne permet encore de déceler si celle-ci
voyage ou s'instruit beaucoup. Ou du moins, si
elle aime le faire. Et nous rapportons toujours
des souvenirs de nos voyages, guidés par notre
envie d'exotisme ou dans l'espoir de conserver
une émotion appartenant désormais au passé.
Dans les intérieurs que nous avons sélectionnés
pour cet ouvrage, les objets collectionnés ont pas
mal de kilomètres au compteur. Les personnes
qui occupent ces intérieurs sont des nomades
modernes, bien que leur vie ne se résume plus
depuis longtemps à une valise ou un cabinet de
curiosités. Leur habitation est le reflet d'une
destination sans pareille, où l'on peut s'évader
par la pensée. Vos guides pour ce voyage sont
le photographe Jan Verlinde et l'auteur Thijs
Demeulemeester. Enjoy the trip.

PHOTOGRAPHY

Jan Verlinde

TEXT

Thijs Demeulemeester

GRAPHIC DESIGN

Elvire Delanote

FINAL EDITING

Sabine Van Humbeeck (NL)
Blue Lines (FR & EN)

TRANSLATION

Blue Lines (FR)
Joy Philips (EN)

© Jan Verlinde & Thijs Demeulemeester
© Lannoo Publishers, Belgium, 2021
D/2021/45/206– NUR 450/454
ISBN 978 94 014 7743 7
www.lannoo.com

Sign up for our newsletter with news
about new and forthcoming publications
on art, interior design, food & travel,
photography and fashion as well as
exclusive offers and events.

If you have any questions or comments
about the material in this book, please
do not hesitate to contact our editorial
team: art@lannoo.com

Homes   for   Nomads